PROTECTING the EARTH'S ANIMALS

Battling
Wildlife Poachers
The Fight to Save Elephants, Rhinos, Lions, Tigers, and More

DIANE BAILEY

PROTECTING *the* **EARTH'S ANIMALS**

Battling Wildlife Poachers

The Fight to Save Elephants, Rhinos, Lions, Tigers, and More

BY DIANE BAILEY

Mason Crest
450 Parkway Drive, Suite D
Broomall, PA 19008
www.masoncrest.com

Series ISBN: 978-1-4222-3872-1
Hardback ISBN: 978-1-4222-3874-5
EBook ISBN: 978-1-4222-7911-3

First printing
1 3 5 7 9 8 6 4 2

Produced by Shoreline Publishing Group LLC
Santa Barbara, California
Editorial Director: James Buckley Jr.
Designer: Patty Kelley
www.shorelinepublishing.com

Library of Congress Cataloging-in-Publication Data
Names: Bailey, Diane, 1966- author.
Title: Battling wildlife poachers : the fight to save elephants, rhinos, lions, tigers, and more / by Diane
    Bailey.
Description: Broomall, PA : Mason Crest, [2018] |
Series: Protecting the Earth's animals | Includes bibliographical references and index.
Identifiers: LCCN 2017001354| ISBN 9781422238745 (hardback) | ISBN 9781422238721 (series) |
    ISBN 9781422279113 (ebook)
Subjects: LCSH: Poaching–Africa–Juvenile literature. | Poachers–Juvenile literature. | Wild animal
    trade–Africa–Juvenile literature. | Wildlife conservation–Africa–Juvenile literature. | Endangered
    species–Juvenile literature.
Classification: LCC SK36.7 .B35 2018 | DDC 364.16/2859–dc23 LC record available at https://lccn.
    loc.gov/2017001354

Cover photographs: Dreamstime.com/Charlesmasters (tiger); Henri Faure (rhino). Wikimedia (horns).

QR Codes disclaimer:

CONTENTS

KEY ICONS TO LOOK FOR

Words to Understand: These words with their easy-to-understand definitions will increase the reader's understanding of the text, while building vocabulary skills.

Sidebars: This boxed material within the main text allows readers to build knowledge, gain insights, explore possibilities, and broaden their perspectives by weaving together additional information to provide realistic and holistic perspectives.

Educational Videos: Readers can view videos by scanning our QR codes, providing them with additional educational content to supplement the text. Examples include news coverage, moments in history, speeches, iconic moments, and much more!

Text-Dependent Questions: These questions send the reader back to the text for more careful attention to the evidence presented here.

Research Projects: Readers are pointed toward areas of further inquiry connected to each chapter. Suggestions are provided for projects that encourage deeper research and analysis.

Series Glossary of Key Terms: This back-of-the-book glossary contains terminology used throughout this series. Words found here increase the reader's ability to read and comprehend higher-level books and articles in this field.

INTRODUCTION

Even looking from an airplane, hundreds of feet above the ground, it was still easy to spot Satao. He was a "tusker," a kind of elephant known for his enormous tusks. At 6.5 feet (2 m) long and 110 pounds (50 kg) each, the tusks almost dragged on the ground. It was impossible to know for sure, but he might have had the largest tusks of any elephant in the world. Thousands of visitors came to Tsavo East National Park in Kenya just to get a glimpse of Satao. It wasn't just curious tourists who wanted to see him. The famous bull elephant was also a target for poachers. His giant tusks were made of solid ivory. They were worth thousands of dollars.

The park rangers at Tsavo knew this, and they guarded the elephant closely. In the spring of 2014, the rangers went on high alert. Heavy rain had come to the area. Looking for food, Satao had crossed into a dangerous area of the park. It was a prime hunting ground for poachers, but there are only so many rangers, and they just couldn't keep track of him all the time. Poachers attacked in May, shooting poisoned arrows to bring the giant animal down. Then

African elephants depend on the open savanna for a home.

they butchered Satao, cutting off his face to get his tusks.

Authorities found the body a few days later. It was so badly cut up that they did not know for sure it was Satao, but they feared the worst. They sent planes out to look for Satao, hoping to spot him in one of his favorite hangouts. All the flights came back with the same report: No one had seen him. Finally, after a week, they confirmed that the dead elephant was Satao.

Satao was particularly famous, but he was not unique. Thousands of ordinary elephants suffer the same fate. Experts estimate that almost 100 elephants are killed every day by poachers in Africa. That's one every 15 minutes! Rhinoceroses, tigers, lions, leopards, gorillas, and other species are also being targeted. Some of them face extinction. Fortunately, there are people fighting on the other side of this war. They know that stopping poaching won't be easy, but their mission is clear: Find a way.

WORDS TO UNDERSTAND

apex predator a meat-eating animal at the top of the food chain, with no natural enemies

biodiversity the amount of different plants and animals in a certain area

bribe to illegally give someone money in exchange for a favor

ecosystem the places that species live, and how they interact with each other and their environment

savanna a large area of grassland

A KILLER PROBLEM

Imagine standing in the middle of Africa 200 years ago. A huge herd of elephants moves across the **savanna**, visible as far as the eye can see. There are some 26 million of these animals, the largest land mammal in the world, and they rule the continent.

Fast forward 100 years and the scene is much different. Only three to five million elephants remain. People in Asia, Europe, and America want ivory, and there's only one way to get it—from elephants slaughtered for their tusks. In another 50 years, their numbers are down by half again. Today, the population of African elephants has fallen to only about 350,000. The elephants do not rule the savanna anymore.

Poachers do.

Before the 20th century, killing wildlife was generally legal. There was a booming trade in animal parts. People bought elephant ivory, rhinoceros horns, tiger bones, and lion skins. But then the numbers of animals began to fall dramatically. Populations were being wiped out faster than they could rebuild. Laws were passed to limit killing, but it did not solve the problem. Hunting wildlife just moved underground.

Poaching is the act of illegally killing or capturing an animal, and it's big business. Experts think the illegal wildlife trade is worth about $19 billion a year. It's hard to shut down an industry that big. Poaching has already made some species extinct. If it doesn't stop, more may die out soon.

Out of Africa

Poaching occurs wherever humans and animals live together, but the problem is especially bad in Africa. For one thing, Africa is one of the few places in the world that still has significant numbers of large animals like elephants, rhinoceroses, and lions. Africa is also the planet's poorest continent; people may earn only a few hundred dollars a year. Poaching is a way to make money fast. Even though it's illegal, it's often easy to get around the law. The govern-

A park ranger looks over amputated elephant feet.

ments of many African nations are not stable. Poachers can **bribe** corrupt officials, offering them money to ignore their crimes.

There are several poaching "hot spots" in Africa—easy places for poachers to find animals and move goods out of the country without getting caught. The countries of Tanzania and Mozambique in eastern Africa are two of the hot spots. So is the "Tridom" region on the continent's western side, which includes parts of Gabon, Cameroon, and the Republic of the Congo.

Most of the animals poached in Africa do not stay there. The world's main buyers of poached animal goods are located in Asia. In the past, a lot of poaching also occurred in Asia, but by now, poachers have already wiped out most of Asia's bigger animals. They have moved on to the animals in Africa. (Tigers are an exception. They do not live in Africa and are poached in India, China, Indonesia, and Russia.)

Chinese use of animal parts

Healthy and Wealthy

The market for wildlife in Asia dates back thousands of years. A few hundred years ago, before the age of modern medicine, people in Asia relied on traditional cures. They used plants and animal parts to treat everything from headaches to stomach cramps. Rhino horns were thought to help fevers, for example. Tiger bones were considered a good way to fight arthritis. Modern scientific experiments have shown that these treatments are not effective, but many people still believe in them. In the mid-2000s, a rumor began going around in Vietnam saying that rhino horns could cure cancer! The demand for rhinos surged, and poachers went to work. Within a few years, the Javan rhino was wiped out of Vietnam. (A few still live in Indonesia.) The western black rhino from Africa was declared extinct altogether. Rhino horns are made of the same material as fingernails and there is no evidence that they have any effect on cancer. Still, the rumor alone caused major damage to rhino populations.

Many Asian people also see animal products as status symbols. The more rare (and expensive) something is, the more prestige it brings. People may show off their wealth by owning a rhino horn cup, a tiger-skin rug, or a carved ivory statue. They can give them as gifts to impress their friends or business associates. Wealthy customers may

Tiger-skin rugs are just one of many animal status symbols.

also eat the meat of poached animals. An exotic dinner of lion steak or monkey brains can cost hundreds of dollars. That's another source of money for poachers.

Not all poached animals are killed. There is also a thriving pet trade. Buyers may be wealthy individuals who want a pet chimpanzee, gorilla, or even elephant of their own. Zoos are another market. (Legitimate zoos get their

DON'T BE A NUISANCE

You might be used to seeing a rabbit nibbling in the garden or a raccoon sniffing around the trash. They might be a nuisance, but they do not usually cause too much trouble. In Africa, nuisance animals may be much bigger. Elephants can wander through villages, destroying fences and trampling crops. Lions prey on livestock. When these animals get too close, people often kill them before they can cause damage. This is another type of poaching. It's illegal, but people usually don't get in trouble for it. Most of them agree the animals are destructive and should be killed. In 2012, local villagers near Nairobi National Park in Kenya were angry that lions had eaten their goats. They sneaked up on the lions at night, and ran them down with cars. Park rangers saw the incident, but did not step in because they were afraid of the mob.

animals through legal sellers, but there are many smaller ones that do not.)

Although most poached goods are sold in Asia, other countries also contribute to the poaching industry. The United States is a big market for luxury wildlife items, especially ivory. However, in 2016 the U.S. government banned almost all ivory from entering the country. The hope was to bring the demand down and help stop poaching.

Keys to the Kingdom

Most people agree that it is unfortunate if a species goes extinct. Every lost animal means less **biodiversity**. That is an important characteristic of healthy **ecosystems**. Losing any species affects the animals and plants around it. Some of the animals most endangered by poaching are especially vital; the roles they play in the environment cannot be done by any others

In certain kinds of structures, such as an arch, there is a keystone. This one stone supports the entire structure. If it is removed, the arch collapses. The same thing can happen with an ecosystem. Take away one part, and the entire system can fall apart.

Elephants are an example of a keystone species. They

are powerful creatures—no other land animal even comes close to matching their strength. Elephants routinely trample grassland, and they can pull trees out of the ground with their trunks. Believe it or not, this demolition derby is actually good for the environment. It helps keep the grassland open for grazing by other animals like zebras, giraffes, and antelopes. During the dry season, elephants are the only animals strong enough to dig holes to reach water trapped underground. They make small ponds which other animals use to get water, too.

Rhinos are also considered a keystone species. They live

Watering holes are vital resources for African zebras.

on grass, and at 2,000 pounds apiece, that's a lot of grazing. These living lawn mowers help keep the vegetation in check. In turn, that helps reduce the risk of wildfires that could destroy a large amount of habitat. Lots of eating also means lots of pooping. Rhinos help distribute seeds throughout the landscape this way, so that new plants can grow.

Lions and tigers are **apex predators**. That means they are atop the food chain. They hunt whatever smaller animals they want—but nobody hunts them. They might seem like they're taking a lot and not giving back. In fact, the ecosystem has developed to depend on these predators, too, since they keep the populations of smaller animals under control. In turn, that keeps the amount of plants in balance. If smaller animals ate up all the plants, there wouldn't be enough for the larger animals—like elephants and rhinos.

Keeping Things Wild

Africa is an extremely diverse place when it comes to animal species. It's also diverse when it comes to people. The continent has more than 50 countries, and its people speak more than 2,000 languages. Of course, not everyone in Africa has the same goals or priorities. The governments of many African countries recognize that it's

Rhinos are among the most poached African animals.

important to save their species, but not all of them do. They use different approaches to protect their animals, and their success varies.

In recent years, for example, poaching rates have fallen in Kenya and South Africa. On the flip side, things have gotten worse in Mozambique and Zimbabwe. One country might have strict laws against poaching. It's easy for poachers to move to a country that does not, though. Without a joint effort against poaching, scientists think several species are in danger of becoming extinct within just a few years.

Just in the last decade, the western black rhino has become extinct, while the northern white rhino is down to only five individuals. There are only a few thousand tigers left in the wild, down from 100,000. Elephants are dwindling, too, with about 350,000 left. Experts say that if current poaching rates continue, elephants could be extinct as soon as 2020.

It's going to take a lot of creativity and manpower to stop poaching. And it's going to take a lot of money. But if the world starts losing even more species, the price could be much higher.

TEXT-DEPENDENT QUESTIONS

1. How much money is the illegal wildlife trade worth?
2. What is one medical problem people try to treat with rhino horn?
3. Why is a keystone species especially important in an ecosystem?

RESEARCH PROJECT

Read more about apex predators. Make a food chain or food web chart for African savanna areas.

ON THE FRONT LINES

The poachers whiz overhead in small planes, looking for rhinos. It's the dead of night, and the savanna glows an eerie green color through the poachers' night-vision goggles. Their rifles are equipped with silencers.

When they find a rhino, they act fast. First they shoot him with poison darts. The rhino grunts, stumbles, and collapses. The rhino may die; he may not. The poachers don't care. They just want its horn. Using a *panga*, a tool like a machete, they hack the rhino's horn off. It takes less than a minute.

Now for the escape. Will they get out without being caught? Maybe.

Or maybe, like the rhino, they're also being tracked.

Sophisticated Criminals

There is no way to describe a "typical" poacher. Some are local residents who kill animals for food or to protect their property. Others also live in the area, but they're in it for the money. They intend to sell the animal in a commercial market. Farther up the ladder, poaching turns into a huge industry. Poachers are often part of international crime organizations that also deal in other illegal products, like guns and drugs and have built underground networks all over the world. They know where and when to move goods without getting caught, often paying local officials not to turn them in.

Helicopters are used to spot and chase poachers from the air.

That's why it's best if authorities catch poachers *before* they have a chance to strike. It's a tough job. There are hundreds of thousands of square miles of wilderness in Africa. It's impossible to keep an eye on everything. Plus, poachers often

A tour of Zakouma National Park

have better equipment, and a lot more money. Worst of all, they are ruthless, ready to kill people who get in their way or try to stop them. For African park rangers, the leading cause of death is getting killed by poachers.

There are some changes, however. At Zakouma National Park in southeastern Chad, for example, poachers were slaughtering elephant herds in the early 2000s. The government was trying to stop them, but they did not have the expertise or equipment to do it. The poachers had them beat.

In 2012, the government hired a private company to help. The company improved the park's radio system and got GPS devices for the rangers. They built airstrips to make it easier to get in and out of the park quickly and put tags on the elephants. Although there were still some bloody battles between poachers and rangers, the changes helped. Between the end of 2012 and late 2015, no elephants were poached in Zakouma.

THE POACHER AND THE PARK RANGER

In March of 2013, a herd of elephants gathered at Fianga, a wetlands area on the border of Chad and Cameroon in central Africa. It was still the dry season, and the elephants were taking a break. They needed to rest and drink before they moved on during their annual migration. That's when poachers attacked. By the time they finished, 86 elephants lay dead. The poachers had brutally removed their tusks with hacksaws.

A park ranger named Adoum Mahamat Brahim heard about the slaughter. He believed he knew who had done it. It was a poacher named Hassan Idriss Gargaf. Gargaf had grown up near Chad's Zakouma National Park. His family were poor farmers, and Gargaf had earned money as a child leading cattle drives. From that, he also learned how and where elephants traveled. Once Gargaf grew up, he became a poacher, which paid better than herding cattle.

Brahim was the same age as Gargaf, and came from the same area, but he chose conservation over killing. He became interested in elephants as a child. As a teenager he volunteered as a patrol officer. Later he joined the staff at Zakouma, where his path crossed with Gargaf's.

Brahim conducted a **sting operation** in 2011. He pretended to be interested in buying ivory, and tricked Gargaf into meeting him. He found out where Gargaf was hiding and had him arrested. Gargaf went to jail, but the jail had poor security, and Gargaf soon escaped. In 2012, Gargaf was arrested for another poaching crime in Cameroon, but he walked out of that prison, too.

So when Brahim heard about the massacre at Fianga in 2013, he thought of Gargaf. Just as he had two years earlier, Brahim tracked Gargaf down. Authorities raided his house, and the notorious poacher went back to prison.

Meanwhile, the elephant population at Zakouma had been rebounding. There were no poaching incidents in 2012, 2013, or 2014. After years with very few births, 40 calves were born. It gave new hope for the health of the herd, but then, in 2015, poachers struck at Zakouma again. They killed two females and their calves.

Was it Gargaf, out of prison once again, who did it, or was it someone else? The names and faces change, but the battle goes on.

Tech Tools

There's no doubt that poaching is a war, but technology is helping out. For every poacher's gun, there's a gadget that may stop it in time. One new software tool is called Protection Assistant for Wildlife Security—or PAWS, for short. Scientists enter data about where animals have been seen into the computer program. They also put in locations of traps or snares that have been found. Using this information, the program figures out where poachers have been, and where they're likely to strike next, and also draws up patrol routes for rangers.

Patrols can also get help from technology in the field. The Rainforest Connection is a nonprofit company that collects old cell phones. It installs microphones on them, and then places them in trees in the wilderness. The microphones pick up sounds around them, and transmit the signals back to command central, where a computer analyzes the sounds to determine whether they're natural noises. If not, it sends a message to authorities, who can investigate. The devices were originally developed to stop illegal logging, but they can also be used to detect gunshots, which suggest poachers are in the area.

Another technology comes from the World Wildlife Fund

(WWF). It partnered with Google to develop heat-sensitive cameras. The cameras use **infrared** technology to find objects that are producing heat. A software program analyzes the data to determine whether the object is an animal or a human. If it's human—which may mean a poacher—the system alerts park rangers.

Of course, poachers are always on the move, and it's hard for rangers to keep up. That's where drones come in. Several companies fly these unmanned aircraft over the

Microphones left in trees can help track poaching activity.

GORILLA WARFARE

Scientists were in the field in northwestern Rwanda when they spotted a noose attached to a branch in the jungle. It was a poacher's snare, set to trap mountain gorillas. There were gorillas nearby, so one of the researchers started to approach the snare. He wanted to disable it before the gorillas got caught. He never got a chance, though. A grunt from a **silverback** stopped him. The gorilla's message was clear enough: *Stay back. We've got it covered.*

As the researchers and the silverback watched, three young mountain gorillas—two 4-year-olds and a teenager—went to work. Working together, they jumped on the branch to loosen the rope, and then removed it. That was one trap down. Now they moved through the jungle and did the same thing to the next one. The researchers were pleased to see the gorillas learning to protect themselves, because it may be just in time. This critically endangered population is down to fewer than 800 animals.

thousands of square miles that need patrolling. The drones have infrared cameras and other equipment to pick up human activity and report it.

A wildlife journalist named Bryan Christy came up with a creative way to find out what poachers were doing. He had some fake elephant tusks made. They looked just like regular ivory, but inside was a GPS device that could be

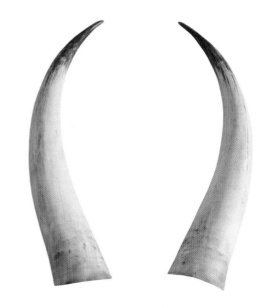

The fake tusks used to trap poachers looked like these real ones.

followed by satellites. Christy was able to track the path of the tusks as they were smuggled around Africa. By seeing where they went, authorities learned that money from poaching was going to help terrorist armies.

No Two Alike

It's not always possible to catch poachers before they get their prey. However, scientists and authorities are finding better ways to figure out where poachers are working. Hopefully, the information will help stop them the next time. In the late 1990s, an American biologist named Samuel

Wasser developed a way to take DNA samples from elephant poop. Soon after, his team figured out how to get DNA from ivory tusks. Put the two together, and they can tell authorities a lot.

Elephant poop, of course, is scattered all over Africa. It's clear evidence of where the animals live and travel. If authorities seize a shipment of illegal tusks, Wasser and his team can test DNA in the ivory and compare it to their "field samples." When they get a match, they can tell where the ivory came from. This helps officials target the areas where poachers are working.

There are also efforts in countries such as Kenya, Nigeria, and South Africa to set up a kind of DNA library. This database is filled with genetic samples from thousands of endangered species. These DNA samples work like price bar codes. Each one matches a specific type of animal. They are stored on a computer and can be compared to animals that are being poached.

Sending a Message

It's one thing to catch a poacher. It's another to **prosecute** him and make sure the crime is punished. Officials are usually law enforcement officers who are used to handling

National rangers train to track and arrest poachers.

crimes against people. They don't have the right skills to look for evidence at a poaching crime scene. For example, sometimes it can be difficult to tell if an animal died naturally or if it was killed on purpose.

Most African countries do not have the money to hire enough people and train them properly, so the United States and other countries are lending a hand. They help pay for programs that teach officials how to run undercover operations, investigate crime scenes, and prosecute poachers.

Even if they are guilty, poachers do not always get in trouble. Sometimes they can bribe officials to let them go. If they do get punished, it might just be a few months in jail

These rangers show off captured rhino horns.

or a fine of a few hundred dollars. In recent years, though, several African countries have made poaching sentences harsher. Kenya changed its laws in 2014 so that poachers face a fine up to about $230,000, and possibly life in prison. Before, the fine was less than $1,000, and there was no jail time. In 2016, Indonesia made plans to increase prison sentences from five years to 20 for poachers. And in 2015, Mozambique passed laws that made poaching punishable by 12 years in jail. That's lighter than in other countries, but before the change, poaching was only a **misdemeanor** in Mozambique.

Poachers are professional smugglers, and stopping them is a big job. However, there is another side to the problem. For every seller, there is also a buyer.

TEXT-DEPENDENT QUESTIONS

1. What are some tools that poachers use?

2. About how many mountain gorillas are left in the wild?

3. What two things does the American biologist Samuel Wasser use to collect DNA samples from elephants?

RESEARCH PROJECT

This chapter has several creative solutions to poaching problems. Go online and see if you can find any others, whether in Africa or other parts of the world.

WORDS TO UNDERSTAND

activist someone who works for a particular cause or issue

parasite an animal that lives completely off of another animal, without giving anything back

tranquilizer a drug used to temporarily knock an animal unconscious

treaty a formal agreement between two or more countries

MANAGING THE MARKET

Ordinary people like businessmen and housewives may not look like criminals. But people who buy products made from poached animals are a big part of the problem. There are international regulations that say which wildlife goods can be sold legally, and which can't. However, buyers do not always understand the rules . . . or they may not care.

Old Ways, New Wealth

The tiger is an important animal in Chinese culture. It is admired for its strength and beauty, and some people think it has special powers. For centuries, Chinese people used tiger bones to treat certain medical conditions. They wore clothes made from tiger skins or used them to make decorative items for their homes. Tiger products were expensive, however. Most regular people could not afford them.

In recent years, China has become a wealthier country. The economy is growing, and there are more people with extra money to spend. That has driven up the demand for tiger products, and caused more poaching.

Ivory figures like this one are highly prized in China.

There's a similar problem with elephant ivory. In 2013, a survey of 600 Chinese people showed that more than 80 percent planned to buy ivory in the future. Almost 90 percent thought that owning ivory was a sign of prestige, but less than 20 percent thought that owning ivory was connected to cruelty to animals. Huge amounts of ivory are imported to China, but only some of it is legal.

It's hard to change traditions, and even harder to change people's minds. Still, many people think the only way to stop poaching is to kill the demand. It's a tall order, but there's one man who might be tall enough to do it. Standing 7'6" (2.3 m), Yao Ming is a famous Chinese basketball player. He played first in China and then later for the Houston Rockets in the United States. In 2012, he started to campaign against elephant poaching. In China, where he is extremely popular, Yao's face went up on billboards that urged people to "Say No to Ivory." (Yao has also worked against rhino poaching.)

In late 2016, for the first time, the Chinese government officially announced that it would shut down the nation's ivory market. The move was cheered by animal rights groups. Most hoped that this will make a big change in the demand for ivory and reduce the harm done by poaching. However, time will tell if the Chinese efforts will be enough.

For example, one worry is that by making ivory harder to buy, it would become more valuable. Also, China is the world's biggest market for poached goods, but it's not the only one. Other countries in Asia, such as Vietnam, Thailand, and Laos, also add to the demand. The United States and nations in Europe create other strong markets for illegal wildlife. The Chinese move was big, but wherever there is money, there is a market.

No Good for Anyone

Making pink rhino horns.

You might love ice cream, but you'd probably skip that hot fudge sundae if you knew it would give you food poisoning. You would not buy a new coat that had been splattered with a gallon of paint. Some conservationists are trying a similar approach with animals. They are trying to make products that come from poached animals worthless. They hope that if people do not want to buy the products, the poachers will stop killing.

In South Africa, men are armed with **tranquilizers**, looking for rhinos. They're not poachers, though. They're wildlife **activists**. They don't have sharp pangas in their backpacks. Instead, they've got poison and pink dye. Their mission? Ruin a rhino horn.

After knocking the rhino unconscious, the activists inject the poison and dye into the rhino's horn. The poison does not hurt the rhino. (In fact, it helps fight **parasites**.) It's not fatal to humans, either. However, it will make them sick with diarrhea and vomiting. The activists hope the poachers will see the unnatural pink color in the horn and know that it has poison in it. Then they might skip over this rhino.

Treating a rhino this way is a lot of work, however. Plus,

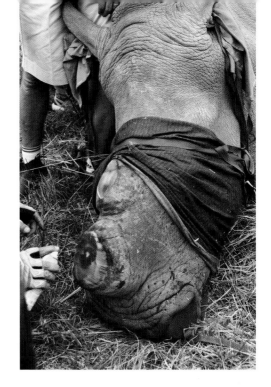

there's always the risk that the rhino could wake up before the procedure is finished! And there are too many rhinos to do this on.

Even if conservationists think the horn is now useless, poachers do not always agree. The dye will eventually fade, and poachers often do not care if the horn has poison in it. They're just selling it to someone else. Buyers do not know they are getting a bad horn.

Removing a rhino's horn might make it safer from poachers.

Another method is to remove the horns altogether. That is also expensive and time-consuming. Plus, it may not work. Poachers may kill the rhinos anyway to make sure they don't waste time tracking the same rhino again. Still, there is some evidence that de-horning can help. Over the last few years, de-horned rhinos in Zimbabwe and South Africa were less likely to be poached. If conservationists can save even a few rhinos this way, it may be worth it.

Making Things Legal

It is fairly simple to pass a law making it illegal to buy or sell poached goods. Enforcing it is much more difficult. In China, for example, there is a long tradition of ivory carving. Some of the country's ivory supplies are legal to use. However, the legal trade is often a way to cover up the illegal trade. It's a problem to distinguish between what is legal and what isn't.

The Convention on International Trade in Endangered Species (CITES) is a **treaty** that started in 1975 to make

China confiscated this stockpile of illegal, poached ivory.

sure that trade in wildlife products does not threaten the survival of a species. In 1989, many people worried about the dwindling elephant populations. In response, CITES put a worldwide ban on ivory trading. The result was just what they hoped, and trade in ivory dropped dramatically. Over the next 20 years, elephant populations in Africa started to come back.

When the ban went into effect, several African countries had lots of ivory stored up, but the treaty meant that they had nowhere to sell it. In 1999, CITES agreed to a one-time legal sale. The countries of Botswana, Namibia, and Zimbabwe were allowed to sell their ivory to Japan. A similar sale happened in 2008. That ivory was sold to Japan and China. The money from the sales would go to elephant conservation efforts. The plan did not quite work. All of a sudden, there was a flood of ivory onto the market. It did not satisfy people's demands. It only made them want more. The market for illegal ivory started getting bigger.

A similar thing happened with tigers. In the early 1990s, the Chinese government helped create an industry for tiger farming. The idea was to raise tigers in captivity and then reintroduce them into the wild. That would help bring population numbers back up. However, tigers raised in

GUILT-FREE IVORY?

If an elephant is alive, taking its tusks is a cruel act. But what about taking the tusks of an elephant that has died naturally? Some people argue that the poaching

problem could be helped by establishing a legal trade in this "guilt-free ivory." The idea has some problems. For one thing, it would depend on having a large number of elephants to start with. Right now, the number of elephants is going down, not up. It would also mean a lot of effort devoted to looking for dead elephants. Rangers would have to harvest their tusks before the weather ruined them. Once this ivory went to market, it would still be difficult to determine if it was legal. Poachers could use this gray area to harvest the tusks of live animals. However, if this ivory could be sold legally, it could provide money to help protect elephants from poachers.

captivity do not survive in the wild. Now, many tigers are raised simply so their parts can be sold as luxury items to wealthy Chinese citizens. Farmed tigers cannot keep up with the demand, however, so poachers also hunt wild tigers.

Trophy Hunting

In most of Africa, it is illegal to kill endangered species, but there are some exceptions. "Trophy hunting" is a legal industry in several places. Hunters pay for the right to hunt animals, as long as the animals do not live in a protected area. In Zimbabwe, hunters can hire guides to help them track and shoot a lion. South Africa has the largest trophy-hunting industry in the world, mostly focused on rhinos and buffalo.

People in favor of trophy hunting say that it can help preserve endangered populations. It costs a lot to buy a trophy hunt, sometimes more than $200,000. The idea is to put the money toward conservation efforts. Supporters also say that only a certain number of animals is allowed to be hunted, so it won't hurt the overall population.

Opponents of trophy hunting argue that hunting endangered animals is not a good idea. It's easy for money to end up in the hands of corrupt officials or guides.

Hunters pay big money for a chance at "trophy" animals.

Also, if hunting endangered species is legal sometimes, then it's harder for authorities to know when it's happening illegally. In South Africa, only about 100 rhinos are allowed to be taken through trophy hunts each year. One rule is that the horn must stay in one piece. That's to prevent it being ground up and sold as "medicine." But this legal hunting can be used as a cover for illegal activity.

A possible compromise is to allow the hunting of big-game animals that are not threatened, such as zebras or giraffes. If hunters follow the rules, the numbers of these animals could still remain healthy. And if the fees go to help local communities, residents would be motivated to preserve wild land for animals.

Trophy hunting does not always work as planned. In 2015, an American hunter traveled to Africa to hunt a lion. He got one, but it turned out to be Cecil, a lion that lived on a reserve. After Cecil's death, people all over the world were outraged. There are probably only about 20,000 lions left in the world. People thought Cecil's death was an example of how trophy hunting encourages a "culture of killing." If some killing is permitted, it makes poaching seem less serious. Unfortunately, that's exactly what endangered species don't need.

TEXT-DEPENDENT QUESTIONS

1. What famous Chinese man has campaigned against elephant poaching?
2. What two things do activists put in rhino horns to stop poachers?
3. What country has the most trophy hunting?

RESEARCH PROJECT

Write a pros and cons chart on the issue of trophy hunting.

WORDS TO UNDERSTAND

census an organized survey designed to count the number of people or animals in a particular place

confiscated taken by authorities as a punishment

ecotourism a type of travel focused on seeing the environment, and protecting it

AN UNCERTAIN FUTURE

When an asteroid hit the earth 65 million years ago, it killed off the dinosaurs and many other species. Scientists call it a mass extinction. Now they warn that the planet may be facing another mass extinction. This time, it will be people's fault.

Thousands of animals are poached every year. Countless more are threatened by habitat loss caused by humans. Large animals, especially, tend to breed slowly, so their natural reproduction rates can't keep up with the losses. Put simply, the current system isn't working. On the positive side, the efforts being made to change things could do the trick—if we do them in time.

Who's Next?

The poaching problem with elephants, rhinos, and tigers is talked about a lot, but they are not the only animals in danger. Zebras are illegally hunted for their meat and skins. Of the three known species of zebras, two are threatened. Poachers also hunt giraffes, usually for their tails. They are seen as status symbols or lucky charms in some African cultures. Since the year 2000, the number of giraffes has dropped by about half, to 80,000. A century and a half ago, there were probably about two million. With most conservation directed at other animals, not much has been done to protect species that are not yet in extreme trouble.

Those species could get that way, however, if steps aren't taken soon. Officials in places like Ethiopia and the Democratic Republic of the Congo have begun counting their remaining animals. They are also putting electronic collars on them, so they can track where they move and shield them from poachers. In the mid-1990s, one giraffe subspecies in the country of Niger was down to only 50 animals. By keeping close watch, though, rangers were able to protect the remaining animals. Now, that population is up to about 200.

One of the rarest animals in the world is the saola. Scientists did not even discover it until 1992. They found

THE PANGOLIN: POACHING'S "MOST POPULAR"

Some people think it looks like a miniature dragon, or maybe a petite dinosaur. How about a cross between an artichoke and an armadillo? A pineapple and a pine cone? Everyone sees something a little bit different in the pangolin. It's cute and ugly at the same time, and it's extremely popular with poachers. Experts think this quirky little mammal may be the most-poached animal of any in the world. Native to certain parts of Asia and Africa, the pangolin is hunted for its meat, as well as its scales and blood, which are used in traditional Chinese medicine. It's difficult to say how many pangolins are killed by poachers. Authorities discover about 10,000 each year, but the actual figure is probably much higher. Several species of pangolin are already endangered. If the poaching does not stop, they could become extinct.

it living in the mountains between Laos and Vietnam. The saola looks like an antelope and is sometimes called the "Asian unicorn." It actually has two horns (not one, like a unicorn) but it seems as hard to spot as the mythical unicorn. The saola is critically endangered. It is getting killed by poachers—and the poachers don't even want it! Saolas get caught in traps that poachers set for other animals, like monkeys and tigers.

Between poaching and other problems like habitat loss, several animals are teetering on the brink of extinction.

Drawing Lines

Take even one piece out of a puzzle, and it ruins the entire picture. Take out several pieces, and it can be almost unrecognizable. That's what is happening to the landscape in much of Africa.

In the past, millions of square miles were covered by large stretches of savanna or jungle. People have changed all that. Like everywhere else in the world, the number of people in Africa is growing—but there's the same amount of real estate. Bit by bit, wild lands are being taken over to plant crops or graze cattle, and logging is another problem. These activities reduce the amount of natural habitat for wild animals. It also makes them more vulnerable to poachers. Places that were once remote now have roads leading into them. Poachers can get in and out faster and more easily.

Building roads and railroads also splits a habitat into pieces. Animals that are used to using certain walking paths or specific

Tsavo West is one of many wildlife preserves in Africa.

routes for migrating can find themselves blocked off. They get stuck in smaller areas, which makes it easier for poachers to find them.

It's not all bad news, though. Much of Africa's wild lands are now protected. They have been turned into national parks and game preserves. It is illegal to build things on these lands, or to hunt there. That won't stop poachers, but it makes it a little easier on rangers, as it's less difficult for them to patrol smaller areas. If they know where animals are living—and where poachers might try to attack—they can do a better job guarding them.

Ripple Effects

Elephants do not look anything like humans. Maybe that's why it's surprising that their behavior can be very similar to ours. Elephants are social animals with families. They play together and help each other out. When one dies, they grieve. More and more, scientists are seeing another elephant emotion: stress.

When their families are being killed by poachers, elephants become so upset that they stop mating. That's a big problem considering that elephants are slow breeders to begin with. Even though elephants can live for 60 to 70 years, a female usually only has about four calves in her lifetime. Unfortunately, poachers work a lot faster than that.

The numbers are bad enough by themselves, but there's more to the story. Poachers don't just kill animals; they

Elephant families can be devastated by the effects of poaching.

disrupt the natural chain of events. Animal families are broken up. The number of males to females gets thrown out of balance. With lions, for examples, poachers usually target the big ones, with the impressive manes, the adult males. If a

Lion poaching news.

poached lion was the head of his pride, the next lion in line steps in. This new lion wants to show he's in charge now. To do that, it's typical for him to kill any cubs that belonged to the previous lion. The death of the first lion now results in many more. Poachers also usually do their work on the borders of national parks, where it's easiest to get to animals. When they kill a lion in that area, another one comes to fill the void, which just gives poachers another target.

#WorthMoreAlive

Huge piles of ivory dotted the landscape at Nairobi National Park in Kenya in April 2016. They came from the tusks of some 6,500 elephants, and weighed about 105 tons. This amount of ivory was worth more than $100 million, but it would never be sold. Instead, the ivory was burned. The president of Kenya, Uhuru Kenyatta, believed this action was worth more than selling the ivory. "Ivory is worthless unless it is on our elephants," he said.

It was not the first time a government had burned ivory that had been **confiscated** from illegal shipments. Other countries have done the same thing over the last several decades, trying to make a point, but Kenya's burn was the largest ever. The event was meant to raise awareness of the poaching crisis in Kenya and throughout Africa. It even came with its own social media hashtag: #WorthMoreAlive.

From an environmental standpoint, those words are certainly true. Elephants, rhinos, and other animals are vital to ecosystems throughout Africa.

Kenya burned a huge pile of poached ivory as a warning to criminals.

Working Together

Poaching involves international gangs, but the bosses behind these crimes need someone to do their dirty work. The "hit men" who do the actual shooting are usually local residents. It's important to make sure local people

 **COUNT ON THIS**

For two years, from 2014 to 2016, researchers conducted the "Great Elephant **Census**." Crisscrossing the entire continent in small planes, they did a survey to count all the elephants in Africa. Some of the news was discouraging. They found a lot fewer elephants than they expected. More than half of Tanzania's elephants had died at the hands of poachers in the five years before the survey, while Mozambique had lost almost that many. However, there were certain areas where elephant populations were growing. What was going on?

The census showed that the countries losing the most elephants were ones with unstable governments that were less able to control poaching. On the other hand, countries such as Botswana, Namibia, and Uganda have stable governments and strict rules about poaching. There, the elephant populations were growing. One reason for Uganda's big spike was that elephants were arriving from the war-torn countries of South Sudan and the Democratic Republic of the Congo. It seems that the elephants had figured out the safest places to live.

have a stake in what happens to animals.

One solution is **ecotourism**. Tourists from all over the world visit Africa to see its magnificent wildlife. If the animals disappear, the tourists will stop coming. In the past, money from tourism usually went only to the companies that ran the tours. Now there are efforts to put some of that money back into the communities themselves. If people who live in these areas benefit from having live animals, they are more likely to protect them.

This approach has been successful in Kenya. The Northern Rangelands Trust is a partner of the international conservation organization The Nature Conservancy. Together, they established 27 wildlife conservation areas in Kenya that are all managed by local communities. From 2012 to 2015, elephant poaching fell 35 percent on those lands.

Tourism can be a moneymaker, but it's also important for people to care about animals even if they don't bring in money. Traditionally, many native cultures in Africa have positive relationships with animals. They respect them for their power, and only kill them when necessary. But with more pressure from the outside world, those relationships have gotten strained. It's possible to bring them back, though.

Animals often fight to establish their territory. To stop poaching, people are going to have to do the same thing. That does not mean taking more land away from animals. It means making a

Safely watching animals might help people appreciate them.

place where people and animals can live together. Their territory and ours are connected, just as it should be.

TEXT-DEPENDENT QUESTIONS:

1. How are saolas in danger from poaching?

2. Why do researchers believe that more elephants have moved into Uganda?

3. What tradition do young men in the Masai tribe go through as part of growing up?

RESEARCH PROJECT

Read about the Masai people of Africa and their relationship with lions. How can that help lions survive?

Get Educated. You can't care about a problem if you don't know about it. Take the time to learn more about how poaching affects animals, their environments, and the people who live in those areas. The more informed you are, the better you can come up with ways to help.

Keep Your Eyes Open. Poachers operate all over the world, and stopping them requires help from everyone. Although large animals from Africa get a lot of the attention, there are also issues with  birds, snakes, turtles, fish, and many other species. In the United States, poaching is a problem with bears, cougars, bighorn sheep, and other animals. If you discover or hear about a problem, contact the police.

Sign Up. Making your opinions known is one of the best ways to get things to change. When thousands of people all say the same thing, governments and other organizations are more likely to listen and take action. There are petitions circulating online to help stop poaching and other wildlife crimes. Signing one does not take much time, and it's a way to make your voice be heard.

Don't Go Wild. You probably weren't going to go buy an ivory figurine or a rhino horn, but just in case—don't. Sometimes it's tough to tell what products are made out of, however, especially if you buy them from small sellers (and especially on the Internet). Educate yourself about where things come from so you can buy responsibly.

Volunteer. You don't have to go to Africa to help the animals there. You can host a fundraiser anywhere—at your school, church, or among your friends. Then, donate the money to an organization that works to fight poaching or conserve wildlife and their habitats. Also, check out some of the many organizations devoted to helping wildlife to find out other ways to help.

Use Your Skills. Do you have good wilderness instincts? A knack with animals? Are you a computer whiz? Whatever your skills, they can be used in a career to help stop poaching. It might be developing a new technology or working in law enforcement, for example. Figure out what your talents are, and think about how you can use them in the fight against poaching.

FIND OUT MORE

BOOKS

Blewett, Ashlee Brown. *National Geographic Kids Mission: Lion Rescue: All About Lions and How to Save Them.* Washington D.C.: National Geographic Children's Books, 2014.

Firestone, Mary. *Top 50 Reasons to Care about Elephants: Animals in Peril.* New York: Enslow Publishers, 2010.

O'Connell, Caitlin and Donna M. Jackson. *The Elephant Scientist.* New York: HMH Books for Young Readers, 2016.

Shea, Nicole. *Poaching and Illegal Trade.* New York: Gareth Stevens, 2014.

Talbott, Hudson. *Safari Journal: The Adventures in Africa of Carey Monroe.* New York: HMH Books for Young Readers, 2013. (Editor's note: Fiction with nonfiction elements)

WEBSITES:

www.iapf.org/
The International Anti-Poaching Foundation sponsors a "green army" whose members learn how to be anti-poaching rangers. Its website has ways young people can help.

www.traffic.org/
Learn how the markets for poached animals work, and find out more about the iconic animals targeted by poachers, such as elephants, rhinos, and apes.

wwf.panda.org/wwf_news/?199903/Stopping-poaching
Read about the current situation with poaching and what WWF is doing to help, and watch a video of an ex-poacher who became a conservationist.

acidification the process of making something have a higher acid concentration, a process happening now to world oceans

activist someone who works for a particular cause or issue

biodiverse having a large variety of plants and animals in a particular area

ecosystem the places where many species live, and how they interact with each other and their environment

habitat the type of area a particular type of animal typically lives in, with a common landscape, climate, and food sources

keystone a part of a system that everything else depends on

poaching illegally killing protected or privately-owned animals

pollination the process of fertilizing plants, often accomplished by transferring pollen from plant to plant

sustain to keep up something over a long period of time

toxin a poison

INDEX

PHOTO CREDITS

Adobe Images: Maciej Czekajewski 8, kitchbain 10, daseaford 15, mkolesnikov85 16, Paul 18, THP-stock 22, Colette 30, viennaframe 38, xtr2007 46, Duncan Noakes 54. AP Photos: Ben Curtis 33, Dennis Farrell 34. Dreamstime.com: cathywithers 20, kamonrutm 36, Svetlana Foote 44, Antonella865 53, Alexander Shamalov 59, pictureguy66 60. Newscom: Europics 42, David Higgs/Balance/Photoshot 48. Rainforest Connection: 28. Shutterstock: Katiekk, 13, simon-g 24, RPSP 26, My name is a boy 31, snap2art 41, Moolkum 51. Tsavo Trust: 6. Wikimedia: Mwangi Kurubi 56.

ABOUT THE AUTHOR

Diane Bailey has written dozens of nonfiction books for kids and teens, on topics ranging from sports to science. She has two sons and lives in Kansas.